Most Outrageous Heists

Jack Booth

Series Editor
Jeffrey D. Wilhelm

Much thought, debate, and research went into choosing and ranking the 10 items in each book in this series. We realize that everyone has his or her own opinion of what is most significant, revolutionary, amazing, deadly, and so on. As you read, you may agree with our choices, or you may be surprised — and that's the way it should be!

an imprint of

■SCHOLASTIC

www.scholastic.com/librarypublishing

A Rubicon book published in association with Scholastic Inc.

Ru'bicon © 2007 Rubicon Publishing Inc.
www.rubiconpublishing.com

Associate Publishers: Kim Koh, Miriam Bardswich
Project Editor: Amy Land
Editor: Joyce Thian
Creative Director: Jennifer Drew
Project Manager/Designer: Jeanette MacLean
Graphic Designer: Deanna Bishop
Editorial Consultant: Police Constable Richard Rand

The publisher gratefully acknowledges the following for permission to reprint copyrighted material in this book.

Every reasonable effort has been made to trace the owners of copyrighted material and to make due acknowledgment. Any errors or omissions drawn to our attention will be gladly rectified in future editions.

"Gangs Target the Weak Spot" (excerpt) by Jonathan McCambridge and Deborah McAleese. From *The Independent*, January 12, 2005. © Independent News & Media.

Cover image: Brink's criminals–corbis; Newspaper–Shutterstock; All others–Istockphoto

Library and Archives Canada Cataloguing in Publication

Booth, Jack, 1946-
    The 10 most outrageous heists/Jack Booth.

Includes index.
ISBN 978-1-55448-486-7

    1. Readers (Elementary) 2. Readers—Theft.
I. Title. II. Title: Ten most outrageous heists.

PE1117.B6612278 2007   428.6   C2007-900574-8

1 2 3 4 5 6 7 8 9 10   10   16 15 14 13 12 11 10 09 08 07

Printed in Singapore

Contents

How Dare They!

You read about them in the papers, and they make for exciting footage on TV — a bank robbery one day, a heist at a jewelry store the next. Do you ever wonder who did it? Or how they knew so much about their target (something the criminals call "casing the joint")? Or what kind of planning went into it? And whether the bad guys will be caught?

Robberies happen every day in all parts of the world. But what makes some heists especially offensive, shocking, or despicable? From incredible targets to unbelievable loots, from impossible break-ins to sensational getaways, the heists that we've collected for our list are the boldest and most outrageous we know of. Some are violent, others shock even security experts and the police, and still others threaten to endanger the lives of innocent people. All crimes are bad, but these 10 are especially shocking.

Whatever you call them — heists or thefts, robberies or burglaries — here are the 10 most outrageous of them all. Hold onto your socks, mind the security alarm, and let's start counting 'em down!

Note: Most of the images in the chapter introductions do not depict actual persons or events. They were created by the artist, unless otherwise noted.

What is the most OUTRAGEOUS HEIST of all time?

A real look inside the Archaeological Museum of Ancient Corinth, which houses a wealth of Greek antiquities from years of excavations in the area.

ITIES LOOTING

DATE: April 12, 1990

TARGET: Archaeological Museum of Ancient Corinth in Greece

THE CRIME: Four robbers used force and violence to break into a museum, and then looted its irreplaceable collection of ancient artifacts.

THE LOOT: At least 285 items believed to be worth more than $430 million

What do you think of treasure raiders like Hollywood's Indiana Jones and Lara Croft? If what they do seems cool to you, think again. In the real world, there's nothing glamorous or heroic about stealing ancient artifacts.

The black market for antiquities is a thriving trade today, thanks to criminals who have no shame. They won't hesitate to steal a piece of history if they think they can make a quick buck on it.

And that's exactly what four robbers did one April night in 1990 — they ransacked an archeology museum in old Corinth, in southern Greece. They came in the middle of the night and stole hundreds of Greek and Roman relics. From marble sculptures to ceramic figures, vases to lamps, all the stolen items were irreplaceable and priceless. Every item had great cultural and historical value and was worth much more than what the robbers could get for selling them.

This thoughtless heist kick-starts our list at #10 ...

---

antiquities: *objects that date from ancient times*
relics: *objects surviving from a culture or period that is no longer around*

CASING THE JOINT

The Archaeological Museum of Ancient Corinth is one of the richest and most significant museums in Greece. It houses thousands of ancient artifacts dug up from the region around it. At the time of the 1990 robbery, it had no alarm system and only one unarmed night guard.

 Why do you think the museum was so lightly guarded? Explain your answer.

THE PLAN

The robbers came in the middle of the night. Unable to break in through the bronze outer doors, they climbed onto the roof. They forced open a skylight and got into the courtyard. When they encountered the lone guard, they brutally attacked him and tied him up. They then went into the museum's two main display rooms, the Greek and Roman galleries. They took what they could carry and loaded the loot into a large truck. Before leaving, they also stole more than $3,000 worth of cash.

THE GETAWAY

The robbers had already disappeared by the time the guards on morning shift arrived. The museum's curators alerted the police and airport authorities about the heist right away. However, the robbers still managed to sneak the stolen goods out of Greece and into the United States.

Quick Fact

In the 1990s, Greece reported more than 30 serious cases of antiquities theft. According to archeologists and police, there's hardly an area in Greece that hasn't been looted by antiquities thieves.

The Expert Says...

"[This crime] highlights once again the real nature of the illicit trade in antiquities. It is not a game for loveable rogues and adventurers: it is a dirty business."

— Neil Brodie, coordinator of the Illicit Antiquities Research Centre, University of Cambridge

illicit: *unlawful*

10   **9**   **8**   **7**   **6**

Recovering the Relics

Though it took more than nine years, the police eventually recovered almost all of the stolen items. Read this report to find out how!

Right after they found out about the heist, the museum's curators sent out an alert with descriptions and photos of everything that was stolen. Alas, years went by with no sign of the robbers or the relics.

Then, late in 1997, five of the stolen pieces showed up at the auction house Christie's in New York! The true payoff for police came in September of 1999. A man who knew the robbers told the FBI that the relics were stored in a warehouse in Miami, Florida.

The FBI and Greek police followed the tip and found 274 of the stolen relics. They were hidden inside 12 crates of fresh fish awaiting shipment!

The police on the case believed that the robbers stored the relics because they had not been able to sell them. It just goes to show — crime doesn't pay!

JUNE 2000

FBI arrested Wilma Sabala who sold five of the relics through Christie's. She was later sentenced in New York to one year in jail.

JANUARY 2001

Greek police arrested Anastasios Karahalios who organized and carried out the robbery. He was later sentenced to life in prison — the harshest sentence ever given for an archeologically related crime.

Quick Fact

There are archeological sites all across Greece. Archeologists are hoping to find ancient cultural relics dating back more than 3,000 years buried in the ground.

Quick Fact

Ancient relics are considered "priceless," because they are irreplaceable pieces of evidence of a city or country's past. They are important for archeologists and historians, because they tell us many things about ancient cultures and the people who made them.

Take Note

This museum looting was much worse than the average robbery. By stealing irreplaceable treasures of archeology and history, the robbers were committing a crime against Greek cultural heritage. This shocking and outrageous act takes the #10 spot on our list.
• What's the most valuable thing in your life? Is it priceless or irreplaceable? What do you do to protect it?

5   4   3   2   1

9 HACKING INTO

A group of criminal hackers tried to steal money directly from a bank's computer system.

SUMITOMO

DATE: October 2004

TARGET: Sumitomo Mitsui Banking Corporation's European head office

THE CRIME: Computer-savvy criminals hacked into a major bank's computer system with the help of an inside man!

THE LOOT: Almost $400 million

In October 2004, a crew of high-tech burglars stunned cops and bankers with their grand plot. They tried to steal almost half a billion dollars from one of the world's largest banks by hacking into its computer system!

The plot sounded like it came straight out of *Mission: Impossible.* People on the inside helped bypass security; criminal hackers waited on the outside for top secret access information; and multiple secret bank accounts were set up around the world to electronically receive the stolen money.

This daring heist would have set the record for the biggest robbery in Britain. But it was stopped at the last minute by a unit of cyber crimes investigators. Even they described the plot as "sophisticated deception."

Read on to find out why we ranked this hacking #9 on our list of most outrageous heists ...

_____

bypass: *avoid something by going around it*

CASING THE JOINT

The target of this heist wasn't just some tiny bank branch — it was the European head office of Sumitomo Mitsui Bank, the second largest bank in the world! This one office in London, England, handles nearly $2 billion worth of money. Its long list of customers includes large corporations and even other banks. The bank's server holds all the top secret information for these accounts, so it has to be locked up in a tightly secured room. Guards patrol the building 24 hours a day and surveillance cameras record everything that moves. This is one secure bank.

THE PLAN

The crew allegedly bribed a security guard into helping them. Not only did he let them in, he turned off the security cameras as well. This meant that the crew would be able to go about the office completely unchecked. Once inside, they attached keystroke loggers onto computers that belonged to the bank workers responsible for money transfers. The loggers would record all the passwords and account details they needed. With these loggers in place, they just went back into hiding and waited. Their trap was set.

THE GETAWAY

After months of secretly logging everything the bank workers typed, the burglars were ready for the big payoff. They hacked into Sumitomo's money transfer system and began the final step in their plan: move close to $400 million into 10 accounts around the world. But the money didn't actually get anywhere — the transfers were stopped just in time by a cyber crimes police unit.

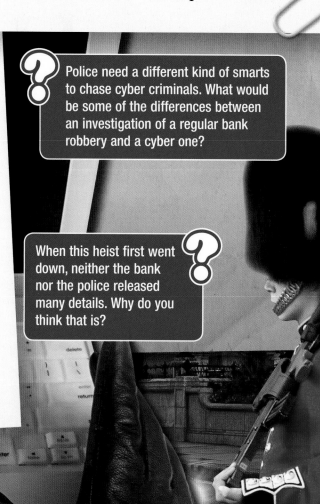

? Police need a different kind of smarts to chase cyber criminals. What would be some of the differences between an investigation of a regular bank robbery and a cyber one?

? When this heist first went down, neither the bank nor the police released many details. Why do you think that is?

Quick Fact

A keystroke logger keeps a record of everything that is typed on the keyboard to which it is attached. To prevent another cyber attack, Sumitomo Bank and others superglued the keyboard connections on their computers!

The Expert Says...

"We have been talking about the doomsday scenario for quite some time and while this [burglary] was not actualized it shows the magnitude of the threat to companies."

— Richard Starnes, president of the Information Security Services Association

CRIMINAL HACKING BY THE NUMBERS

In this information age we live in, many of us are buying things or even banking online. This only makes it more worthwhile for criminals to commit their crimes online too. This fact chart will show you how serious a problem criminal hacking really is.

$400 billion — Cost of damages from computer crimes in the U.S.

1 million — Credit card numbers that have been stolen in Eastern Europe

64% — Percentage of large companies who have suffered losses from hackers' activities

97% — Percentage of cyber crimes that go unreported

$10 million — Amount of money stolen by a hacker group when they hacked Citibank in 1994

350,000 — Credit card numbers stolen from the online music company CD Universe in January 2000. The hacker then tried to force the company into paying him money for "returning" the card numbers, but when executives refused, he posted all of the information on the Web.

$87,000 — Amount of money two hackers from China stole in 1998 after breaking into a bank's computer network. They were sentenced to death after being caught.

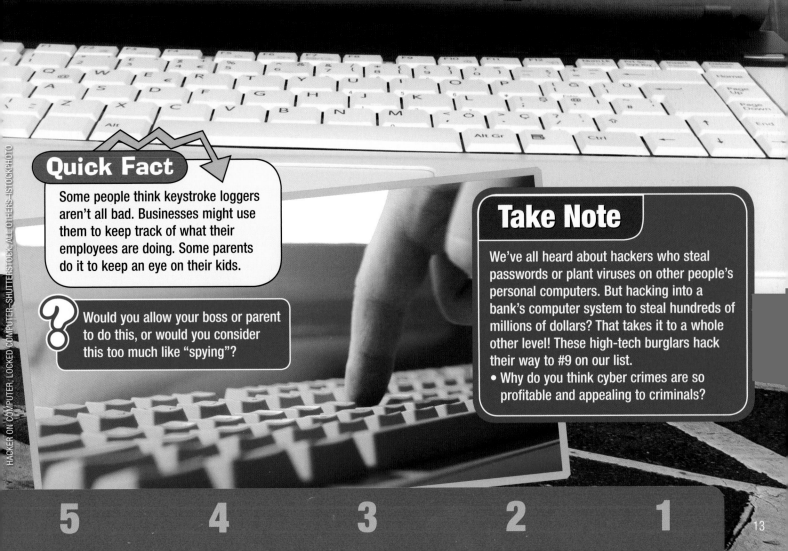

Quick Fact

Some people think keystroke loggers aren't all bad. Businesses might use them to keep track of what their employees are doing. Some parents do it to keep an eye on their kids.

? Would you allow your boss or parent to do this, or would you consider this too much like "spying"?

Take Note

We've all heard about hackers who steal passwords or plant viruses on other people's personal computers. But hacking into a bank's computer system to steal hundreds of millions of dollars? That takes it to a whole other level! These high-tech burglars hack their way to #9 on our list.
• Why do you think cyber crimes are so profitable and appealing to criminals?

HACKER ON COMPUTER: LOCKED COMPUTER–SHUTTERSTOCK; ALL OTHERS–ISTOCKPHOTO

5   4   3   2   1

13

8 SPEEDBOAT

Three museum robbers got away by escaping into the night in a speedboat.

GETAWAY

DATE: December 22, 2000

TARGET: Swedish National Museum in Stockholm, Sweden

THE CRIME: Three robbers used weapons to threaten security guards and bombs to distract police — this was all so that they could get away with their valuable loot by speedboat!

THE LOOT: Three paintings worth more than $30 million

For more than two centuries, the Swedish National Museum had been able to count itself as one of the lucky few in the world of art museums. Even with art crime on the rise, it could still hold tightly to the claim of never having been robbed after years of being open to the public.

But this was all shattered on December 22, 2000. That night, three masked and armed robbers burst into the museum near closing time. It took them only a few minutes to make off with three paintings valued at $30 million. Apart from their high value, these artworks were also Sweden's national treasures!

But the robbers' daring dash into the museum wasn't the only thing to shock police. While the three of them were in the museum, their partners in crime set off two explosions nearby! The mass confusion that followed allowed the museum robbers to slip away into the night.

Quick Fact

Days after the robbery, the police received pictures of the stolen works and a demand for several million dollars in ransom. But none of the paintings were insured by the museum. So museum officials bluntly stated that they had no money to offer in return for the paintings.

CASING THE JOINT

The National Museum in Stockholm is the largest art museum in Sweden. Its painting and sculpture collections alone contain more than 16,000 items. But the art isn't the only thing that attracts visitors to the museum. People come from around the world to marvel at both the museum's magnificent building and its beautiful location — in between two wide waterways, where boats can dock just a few yards from the museum's entrance.

? What do you think was the museum's main security gap?

THE PLAN

After they burst into the museum, one of the robbers stood guard in the lobby. He had a submachine gun with him to keep the museum security at bay, while his two partners ran off to steal the paintings. These two knew exactly where to go and had brought clippers to cut the steel wires that held the paintings in place. At this time, two cars exploded on two separate streets nearby — this dangerous move was part of the robbers' plan to divert attention away from themselves as they prepared to make their escape. On top of creating all this confusion, the robbers scattered spikes on the road to further delay their pursuers.

divert: *distract; change focus*

THE GETAWAY

Carrying the three paintings they had just stolen, the robbers jumped into a small speedboat that had been tied to the dock nearby. People standing outside the museum could only watch helplessly as the robbers sped away into the dark. Two hours after the heist, police actually found the getaway boat on the banks of Malar Lake, south of Stockholm. But the robbers were nowhere to be found. Police think they could have disappeared on to any one of the thousands of tiny islands off Stockholm, or into the dense forests that surround the city.

? Between the museum robbery and car bombings, how do you think police decided which problem to address first?

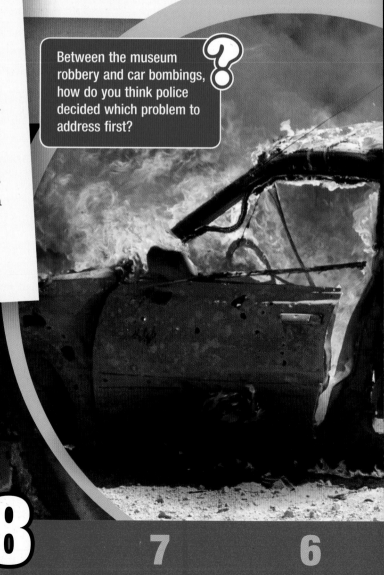

TO CATCH A THIEF

Investigators from Sweden and the United States came together to work on this case. This team effort came after Los Angeles police working on another case found a link between a local criminal group and an organized theft group in Sweden. The global team of investigators discovered that an international theft ring was responsible for the Swedish museum robbery. Check out these quotes to see how police reacted to the outrageous museum heist and those responsible ...

"To have played a part in the recovery of these beloved national treasures of Sweden and indeed of art enthusiasts around the world is most gratifying. ... [We] will continue to develop information with regard to stolen art and strive to achieve the kind of results and success that we see in this case."

— *J.P. Weis, Los Angeles FBI*

"[O]rganized criminal enterprises know no boundaries when embarking in illegal activity. Their activities defy international borders, and reach into the hearts of our local communities. This case illustrates the great lengths these criminals will go to in furtherance of their goals."

— *Sheriff Lee Baca, Los Angeles County Sheriff's Department*

Quick Fact

The police solved this case by pretending they wanted to buy one of the paintings from the robbers. When the robbers showed up in Denmark to sell their stolen goods, they were arrested!

The Expert Says...

"Nobody has any idea as yet who these people are. It was done the same way as when they rob a bank — it was very professional. It seems a bit overdone to use machine guns when you go to a museum."

— Gorel Cavalli-Bjorkman, director of research, Swedish National Museum

Take Note

Submachine guns, car explosions, spikes on the ground, a speedy getaway ... Were you surprised to hear that a group of robbers went to such lengths to steal some paintings? The high drama of this outrageous heist ranks it ahead of the shady hacker job at #9.
• Do you think maybe the police are at fault for letting the robbers get away so easily? Or did they do the right thing by tending to the car bombings first? Explain your answer.

5   4   3   2   1

D.B. Cooper disappeared after his infamous skyjacking.

YJACKING

DATE: November 24, 1971

TARGET: Northwest Orient Airlines, Flight 305

THE CRIME: A bold skyjacker held an airliner and everyone onboard hostage and then disappeared with the ransom money by jumping out of the plane in midair!

THE LOOT: $200,000

On November 24, 1971, a well-dressed man got on a Northwest Orient Airlines flight with nothing but a plain briefcase in his hand. There was nothing remarkable about him — that is, until he revealed that he was hijacking the plane! He demanded a ransom and gave the crew a reason to agree to his terms — he claimed to have a bomb with him!

And when it came time to run, well, let's just say this robber took flight. He jumped out of the back of the airplane with his loot strapped to his chest. And that was the last anyone ever heard from or saw of him, dead or alive.

The police searched far and wide for him, but found nothing. Some people believe he splattered when he landed, or got tangled in the trees and died there. Others believe he survived and pulled off the perfect crime. All we know is that he became known as D.B. Cooper, the original jumping skyjacker!

This outrageous heist — the single unsolved plane hijacking in history — flies in at #7.

CASING THE JOINT

In the early 1970s, airport security was pretty loose. You didn't need to go through any major security checks before you boarded a plane. There were no background checks on passengers, no metal detectors, and certainly no luggage inspection! It wasn't until 1973 that all of these security measures became mandatory.

THE PLAN

Cooper paid $20 cash for a one-way ticket from Portland, Oregon, to Seattle, Washington. Shortly after the plane took off, he pulled out a handwritten note that gave the plane's crew the surprise of their lifetimes. He'd brought a bomb onboard! If they didn't give him what he wanted, upon landing in Seattle, he would set off the bomb and take everyone down with him. The airline had no choice but to agree to the skyjacker's terms: $200,000 and four parachutes. But Cooper wasn't finished yet — he let everyone off the plane (except four crew members) and then demanded that the plane take him to Mexico.

THE GETAWAY

As the plane was heading south somewhere over the wilderness area of the state of Washington, Cooper strapped on his parachute and jumped out of the back of the plane. No one was around when he made his jump. He just disappeared into the night sky, leaving behind just his tie, some cigarette butts, and two of the parachutes.

Quick Fact

Over the past 70 years, more than 500 incidents of air piracy have been reported around the globe. About two-thirds of these happened from 1960 to 1973.

Cooper's bomb ended up being a fake! But of course, neither the airline nor the police knew this at the time. If you were in their shoes, how would you have handled this situation?

Quick Fact

On February 10, 1980, an eight-year-old was digging around a river shore when his shovel overturned a package of money. There was $5,800 inside, all in $20 bills! The FBI confirmed that the money was part of the $200,000 taken by D.B. Cooper. In the 30 years since Cooper escaped, this has been the only solid piece of evidence that police have found.

FBI agents carefully sift through the sand where some of D.B. Cooper's ransom money was found in 1980.

10   9   8   7   6

WANTED!

Was D.B. Cooper a common crook or a "hero" as some people thought? Decide for yourself after you read this report!

D.B. Cooper was charged with air piracy in federal court in 1976, though he obviously never attended court. Even today, the charges still stand and the case is technically still open.

According to the FBI, investigators on the case checked out nearly 1,200 potential suspects! There was enough paperwork from this case to fill an actual Boeing 727 airplane, some say.

When the public found out about Cooper's dramatic heist, some actually thought of him as a "hero."

"[Cooper] took the greatest ultimate risk," explained Dr. Otto Larsen, sociology professor at Washington University. "He showed real heroic features — mystery, drama, romanticism, a high degree of skill, and all the necessities for the perfect crime."

But to the police, Cooper was anything but a hero. He endangered a planeload of passengers, scared the crew, and blackmailed the airline. That made him a criminal.

FBI agent Ralph Himmelsbach spent eight years as lead investigator in this case. He has called Cooper "a rodent," "a dirty, rotten crook," and nothing more than a "sleazy, rotten criminal who jeopardized the lives of more than 40 people for money."

"It's selfish, dangerous, and antisocial," Himmelsbach said once. "I have no admiration for him at all. He's not at all admirable. He's just stupid and greedy."

? Despite the fact that Cooper was a criminal, some people wanted to glamorize his crimes. Why do you think they would make this mistake?

The Expert Says...

"This was a novelty in the annals of skyjacking. Law enforcement was at a loss. They had been drawn beyond the pale."

— John P. O'Grady in "D.B. Cooper, Where Are You Now?"

Take Note

Both the museum heist at #8 and Cooper's skyjacking involved high-speed getaways. But before he performed his famous flying disappearance act, Cooper held a planeload of people hostage. Even though his bomb wasn't real, his threats were! This criminal wasn't a hero — his actions were shockingly unworthy! This earns him and his stunt the #7 spot on our list.

- Do you think a heist like this could happen today? Why or why not?

5   4   3   2   1

Just like the great train robberies of the Wild West, this heist was a daring feat.

CLASS BB18¼

ROBBERY

DATE: August 8, 1963

TARGET: A mail train transporting money from banks in Scotland to London

THE CRIME: A gang of robbers stopped a moving train by posing as railway workers, and then hijacked the cash-carrying cars after threatening to kill the engineer!

THE LOOT: $7 million in untraceable cash (worth over $80 million today)

In a well-hidden safe house, on a secluded farm, miles away from the police, a large gang of robbers began to celebrate. They had just pulled off a huge heist — the biggest robbery in Britain at the time. The loot: more than 120 sacks of cash. It had taken almost a year for this heist to come together, but when it did, the robbers netted what would amount to more than $80 million today.

The Great Train Robbery, as it came to be known, was like a flashback to the days of the Wild West where no train was safe from bandits on horses. But the year was 1963 and the "bandits" were just a bunch of small-time crooks. So how did they manage to pull off one of the most outrageous crimes in British history? Read on to find out …

GREAT TRAIN ROBBERY

CASING THE JOINT

Postal trains heading into and out of London sometimes moved more than just mail — they had special "high value" cars that carried cash and other valuables. One such train was the "Up Special" that ran from Scotland to London overnight. Large amounts of used (in other words untraceable) banknotes were transported to London from various banks. All the money was stored in two cars right behind the engine. The robbers figured out that the Up Special would be carrying a lot more cash than usual the week of August 5 — right after a long weekend holiday for banks in Scotland.

Three hooded men are escorted into a special court in Linslade, Buckinghamshire, England, on August 16, 1963, in connection with the Great Train Robbery.

THE PLAN

The gang sprang into action on August 8, 1963. Around 3:00 AM, they used fake signals to stop the train. A group of "railway workers" (the gang members dressed in bogus blue work clothes) appeared out of the dark and boarded the train swiftly. They separated the rest of the train and hijacked just the cash-carrying cars and the engine. After the gang threatened the engineer with death, he moved the train a few miles ahead toward a bridge. The rest of the gang was already waiting there with their getaway trucks. They quickly formed a human chain and unloaded more than 120 sacks of unmarked bills into Land Rovers they had parked below the bridge.

THE GETAWAY

After looting all the valuables in the "high value" cars, the gang sped away to their safe house in the quiet countryside. They were going to hide out for awhile. When they learned about the massive police hunt for them, they fled yet again. In their hurry, they left behind a ton of evidence for the police.

? The police found the gang's hideout after four days. What do you think police do to find the whereabouts of robbers?

Quick Fact

A Monopoly board and its game pieces became the most famous evidence. Police matched the fingerprints left on these items to criminal records they had on file. Bingo! They knew exactly who to look for.

? If this case were to have played out in the 21st century, the police would be able to use a lot more than just fingerprints. What else would the train robbers have left behind that police could have used as evidence?

CRIMINAL CELEBRITY?

One of the members of the Great Train Robbery gang was Ronnie Biggs. Though he was just a minor player in the heist, he became the most famous of the gang. Read this report to find out why!

After he was arrested, Biggs was sentenced to 30 years in prison. But he escaped in 1965, only 15 months into his term.

Biggs's next step would become as stunning as the robbery itself.

Before he fled the country, he decided he needed to do something about his appearance. The police had released photos of him and his fellow robbers and he didn't want anyone to recognize him and finger him …

So he had plastic surgery!

Biggs moved first to Spain, then Australia, and finally settled in Brazil. Scotland Yard was tracking his every move, but they couldn't do a thing. Britain had no extradition treaty with Brazil, so they couldn't force Brazil to send him back for trial.

In Brazil, Biggs lived the high life — sort of. He had arrived with only £200 (approximately $385) to his name, according to some sources. But no matter, the dough was rolling

Ronnie Biggs leaves Chiswick Police Station on his way to court May 7, 2001.

in. It paid to be the one member of the Great Train Robbery gang who had actually escaped.

For 30 years, Biggs stayed put in Brazil. He even published an autobiography in 1994 called *Odd Man Out*. It contained all the details of the train robbery and became a best seller. Biggs was just showing off, some thought.

Unfortunately, the older Biggs got, the more he missed his homeland. He just wanted to live a normal life and die in the country of his birth.

In May of 2001, Biggs, 72, returned to Britain. The British police arrested him immediately and sent him to Belmarsh Prison to serve his original sentence.

extradition treaty: *agreement between two countries that allows suspected criminals to be sent from one to the other*

The Expert Says…

"Although the operation took all of 15 minutes, the caper was not as smooth as people remember it. It wasn't nonviolent, for one thing … nor was it as carefully executed. …

— Howard Chua-Eoan, *TIME* magazine

Take Note

What made this train-jacking a more outrageous heist than Cooper's skyjacking at #7? Look at how much more was involved in this heist: stopping a speeding train in the middle of its tracks, hijacking the front end, driving off with it, and then hauling away 120 bags of cash. All of these things required perfect timing, planning, and muscle.
• Why do some people treat criminals, such as Ronnie Biggs, like celebrities? Is this appropriate? Why or why not?

5 TEN TON GOLD

The discovery of 76 boxes of gold bars made this heist more dangerous and complicated.

CHALLENGE

DATE: November 26, 1983

TARGET: The Brinks Mat warehouse, near London, England

THE CRIME: A smash-and-grab crew took advantage of a truly golden opportunity to bag tons more loot than they originally planned for.

THE LOOT: Approximately $7 million in cash, $45 million worth of gold, and more than $225,000 worth of diamonds

The original plan was simple. Slip inside the Brinks Mat warehouse and walk out with millions in cash and untraceable traveler's checks. Not a bad haul. Not a spectacular one either though. In fact, by the time they discovered what else they had hit on — by pure coincidence — the originally planned take would seem like chump change. That's because the plain-looking Brinks Mat warehouse held a lot more in store …

And on November 26, 1983, what should the crew of burglars discover in the vault but over 10 tons of pure gold bars sitting in unmarked cardboard boxes!

A simple "smash-and-grab" robbery routine turned into a daredevil heist for the Brinks Mat robbery crew when they decided to go for the gold. They took full advantage of this sudden golden opportunity and now land at the #5 spot on our list.

TEN TON GOLD CHALLENGE

CASING THE JOINT

The Brinks Mat warehouse is located about one mile from Heathrow Airport in London, England. It's a major stopover point for valuable shipments traveling in and out of Heathrow. To keep everything safe, the building is constantly patrolled by a team of security guards, who change shifts early in the morning. Valuables are stored inside a huge vault that can only be opened using two sets of keys and two sets of security codes.

? The timing of a heist is one of the crucial parts of a robbery plan. However, police can exploit these perfectly timed plans, too. Can you figure out how?

THE PLAN

The crew of burglars arrived on the scene at 6:30 AM. They had fake security guard uniforms, which made getting into the warehouse easy. Once inside, they put on masks and made their way to the vault. They overpowered the guards, tied them up, and ordered them to open the vault. Here's where things got really out of hand. The guards, who knew the security code, insisted they couldn't remember it, so the gang poured gasoline over them and threatened to set them on fire unless they revealed the safe's combination. Fearing for their lives, the guards had no choice but to help the gang break into the vault. And that's when the original plan went straight out the window …

THE GETAWAY

The burglars realized that if they were going to steal the boxes of gold and diamonds in front of them, they needed a different approach. First, the gold was heavy, so it had to be moved out of the giant safe with a forklift. The 6,800 bars weighed as much as five small cars put together! Some of the robbers had to leave and come back with larger vehicles to transport the new loot. Almost two hours after they first broke in, the crew finally headed off.

Quick Fact

Originally, the crew's plan was to make this a "smash-and-grab" operation — in and out in five minutes or less. How could they be so sure they could pull this off? They had an inside man! Police later found out it was one of the security guards.

The Mystery of the STOLEN GOLD

It has been more than 20 years since the Brinks Mat gold was stolen. Some of the gold simply vanished into the criminal underworld. Some eventually reappeared in foreign bank accounts around the world. Read this report to find out why police were never able to recover all of the stolen loot.

After the crew escaped with their loot, they realized they had to do something drastic. They knew they couldn't walk around with the gold, or try to hide it, or let it just sit there. Not only were these three options too dangerous, but they also didn't help make the criminals any richer. That's when the crew decided to call in some favors.

Various "specialists" in the criminal world were called in to help melt the gold down into more manageable forms. Only then would the crew be able to sell the gold and make some cold hard cash.

One of the crew's "associates" was a man called Kenneth Noye. Noye was known for his expertise in the gold smelting trade. He would melt down the gold and mix it with other metals like copper. This technique changed the purity of the gold. Now it would be like brand new gold — with absolutely no traces to Brinks Mat left!

The police did manage to seize more than $36 million of the cash that the gang earned from selling some of the gold. They also found 11 bars of the gold in 1985.

After so many years, the police have pretty much given up on finding the rest of the Brinks Mat gold. After the gold went underground, it became impossible to trace its whereabouts. Some people actually think that anyone wearing gold jewelry bought in the UK after 1983 is probably wearing Brinks Mat gold! What do you think?

smelting: *melting a metal, often mixing it with another kind of metal*

 How does this make gold more attractive to robbers than banknotes?

The Expert Says...

 This was a case where collusion with one of the security guards and threats of extreme violence from the robbers led to a highly concentrated police enquiry.

— Alan Wright in *Organised Crime: Concepts, Cases, Controls*

collusion: *agreement on a secret plot*

Take Note

The Brinks Mat burglars used threats and violence to get past a state-of-the-art security system. And they spent hours emptying the warehouse vault. In addition to the 10 tons of gold they stole, they also made off with cash and diamonds! Their outrageous actions and greed combine to earn them the #5 spot on our list.

- This heist took place more than 20 years ago! Could something like this happen today with our new and improved security systems? Why or why not?

5   4   3   2   1

JOSEPH F. McGINNIS

RY BAKER

DNY PI

The actual mug shots of six suspects seized by the FBI in connection with the robbery of Brink's in Boston on January 17, 1950

Criminal

TO BRINK'S

DATE: January 17, 1950

TARGET: A loaded vault belonging to Brink's, a large armored car company

THE CRIME: A gang of professional criminals tried to execute the perfect burglary and almost got away with it.

THE LOOT: Over $2.8 million in cash and checks (over $28 million today)

Every once in a while, we hear about robbers trying to stop an armored car to steal the cash it's carrying. One gang of professional burglars decided to cut to the chase and go straight to the source — rob the armored car company itself.

When the Brink's robbery went down one fateful night in January, 1950, it quickly became known as the "crime of the century." Brink's had once boasted that its headquarters was "burglarproof." Unfortunately, a group of experienced burglars proved that it was anything but!

The heist was a work of criminal genius that took two years to plot and perfect. From the entry to the actual burglary to the getaway, they had it all worked out. For years, the police made no arrests. It seemed like the gang really had gotten away. People began to call this the perfect crime …

CASING THE JOINT

The gang wanted to hit Brink's from the start. Brink's was America's biggest money mover at the time. Its office in Boston had a vault that held vast amounts of money overnight. The gang knew they had to properly case the location. They spent many nights carefully watching the Brink's building, taking notes on exactly what happened when shipments came in, and how many workers were there at night. The gang even did several practice runs so they would know how they would enter the building and ambush the workers.

> How can strict schedules help provide more security for a company? On the other hand, how could they make a company vulnerable?

THE PLAN

On January 17, 1950, the gang decided it was time for the real deal. At 6:55 PM, they pulled up in their truck. Two men waited outside in the getaway truck, while seven entered the building. They had matching outfits from head to toe: navy-style pea coats, chauffeur hats, Halloween masks, gloves, and rubber-soled shoes that would be extra quiet. With keys they had copied on one of their practice runs, they easily went through the front entrance. They snuck up to the second floor and quickly tied up the five workers who were there counting and storing the money collected that day. The gang didn't speak during the entire heist — they had rehearsed so well that each member knew exactly what to do.

THE GETAWAY

At 7:27 PM, the Boston police received a frantic call from one of the workers who had freed himself. The gang had just walked out with their bags of money. By the time the police arrived, the gang was long gone. They had made a quick getaway, hopping right into their waiting truck and driving to a temporary hideout less than six miles away. There, the gang divided the loot and then split!

> The gang had stolen a new truck for their heist. Why do you think they did this?

Boston FBI agents escort two of the six men arrested for this robbery, Vincent James Costa (center) and Michael Vincent Geegan (left), from Federal Court, January 12, 1956.

THE GREAT BRINK'S CONFESSION

The FBI finally solved this case when one of the gang members confessed. Joseph James O'Keefe had been jailed for another burglary when he was cut off by the rest of the gang. Read this official FBI report to find out why this was the perfect time for police to get the lead they needed.

? Why do you think the police choose to talk to suspects when they're isolated from the rest of their fellow criminals?

... From his cell in Springfield, O'Keefe wrote bitter letters to members of the Brink's gang and persisted in his demands for money. The conviction for burglary in McKean County, Pennsylvania, still hung over his head, and legal fees remained to be paid. During 1955, O'Keefe carefully pondered his position. It appeared to him that he would spend his remaining days in prison while his co-conspirators would have many years to enjoy the luxuries of life. Even if released, he thought, his days were numbered. There had been three attempts on his life in June, 1954, and his frustrated assassins undoubtedly were waiting for him to return to Boston. ...

co-conspirators: *people who work together to commit a crime*

Through long weeks of empty promises of assistance and deliberate stalling by the gang members, he began to realize that his threats were falling on deaf ears. As long as he was in prison, he could do no physical harm to his Boston criminal associates. And the gang felt that the chances of his "talking" were negligible because he would be implicated in the Brink's robbery along with the others.

Evidently resigned to long years in prison or a short life on the outside, O'Keefe grew increasingly bitter toward his old associates. ...

At 4:20 PM on January 6, 1956, O'Keefe made the final decision. He was through with Pino, Baker, McGinnis, Maffie, and the other Brink's conspirators who had turned against him. "All right," he told two FBI agents, "What do you want to know?"

For the FBI's entire report on the Great Brink's Robbery, read it online at: http://www.fbi.gov/libref/historic/famcases/brinks/brinks.htm

negligible: *very small*
implicated: *connected to something, such as a crime*

The Expert Says...

" This holdup was very well planned. ... This job was definitely pulled by someone who knew every inch of the company's layout. "

— Edward W. Fallon,
Boston Police superintendent

Take Note

The Boston Brink's robbery edges out the golden heist to take the #4 spot on our list, because of the gang's truly thorough planning. It took six years and the combined efforts of the Boston police, local police departments across the country, and the FBI to crack the case.
• Why does it become harder for police to investigate and solve cases as time goes by?

5   **4**   3   2   1

The Northern Bank robbers held two families hostage in their robbery plot. These innocent victims later described the ordeal as the most terrifying experience of their lives.

NK KIDNAPPING

ALL IMAGES—ISTOCKPHOTO

DATE: December 19, 2004

TARGET: Headquarters of Northern Bank in Belfast, Northern Ireland

THE CRIME: The Northern Bank robbers committed two major crimes — they kidnapped two bank workers and held their families hostage in their plot to rob a bank.

THE LOOT: $50 million

In 2004, just a few days before Christmas, a ruthless gang of robbers broke into the homes of two families in Northern Ireland. They weren't there to rob the families — they were taking them hostage!

The robbers had set their eyes on the Northern Bank headquarters in Belfast, Northern Ireland. But they needed help getting into the bank's vault. So, they went to the homes of two of the bank's executives and held their families hostage. No funny stuff, the ruthless robbers threatened — either help or your family dies. The two bank workers had no choice but to help the dangerous criminals. And that's how one of the biggest cash robberies in history went down.

Read on to find out more about outrageous heist #3 on our list ...

NORTHERN BANK KIDNAPPING

CASING THE JOINT

The Northern Bank is the largest bank in Northern Ireland. Its Belfast location acts as its head office. Here, an underground vault holds all the money that goes through the bank: cash for its 95 branches and hundreds of ATMs, as well as cash deposited by local businesses. The week of the robbery, there was an estimated $58 million in the vault. To keep this money safe, the bank uses a coded dual lock security system for its vault. This means it takes two sets of combinations to open. Only the bank's top executives have access to these codes.

THE PLAN

On the night of December 19, 2004, the gang split up and headed off in two directions. Three of them broke into bank supervisor Chris Ward's home. Two others dressed up as police and conned their way into the home of Kevin McMullan, assistant bank manager. They threatened both men with the same thing: help us break into the bank and your family will be spared. The two bank executives had no choice but to agree. They went back to work the next day as if all was normal. When it came time to close, they stayed behind while everyone else working in the bank went home. It was time to help the robbers get what they wanted.

Quick Fact

Detectives spent days searching the Ward and McMullan houses afterward, looking for clues. But they found nothing. The gang was very careful about not leaving any evidence behind.

THE GETAWAY

The robbers waited outside the bank in their getaway truck the entire time. They didn't even have to enter the bank and risk getting caught. They had instructed the two bank execs to bring out the cash. Bag after bag was passed by the two men to the gang.

? Imagine you were in the position of the two kidnapped bank workers. What would you have done and why?

12-04 L24H
19:45

Security footage showed supervisor Chris Ward leaving the bank the night of the heist. He was carrying a bag that contained more than $2 million.

10   9   8   7   6

GANGS TARGET THE WEAK SPOT ... PEOPLE

A newspaper article from *Belfast Telegraph*

By Jonathan McCambridge and Deborah McAleese, January 12, 2005

With security at bank vaults becoming virtually impregnable, organized crime gangs have realized that humans are the weakest link.

In an increasingly complex criminal world sometimes it is the simplest ideas which work best.

Police intelligence reports and underworld crime gangs share the same use of terminology — a tiger kidnapping is what they both call a crime where a hostage is held to force the victim to take part in a robbery. ...

For years criminal gangs had been frustrated that the improvement in the technology of security at financial institutions had limited their ability to carry out major bank jobs.

---

impregnable: impossible to enter

Highly sensitive alarm systems meant that the days when a robbery gang could crack a safe with a simple explosive device were long gone.

The banks improved their security even further with armored glass, bulletproof shutters, and CCTV cameras. Robbers were reduced to attacking security guards as they made cash deliveries — a much less lucrative and more risky operation.

First London and then Manchester saw a growth in the early 1990s of tiger kidnappings where hostages were taken. Terrified bank, building society, and post office employees were then forced to go to work, where they could nullify the security measures and empty the vaults. The robbers were left with a less risky and more lucrative role — in essence someone else was doing their dirty work for them. ...

---

nullify: *cancel out*
lucrative: *profitable*

The Expert Says ...

"There is a tendency in the aftermath of bank robberies for the focus to be on the amount stolen or the modus operandi of those responsible. It should also be remembered that staff go through a traumatic and stressful experience."

— Larry Broderick, Irish Bankers Officials Association

modus operandi: *method*

Take Note

The Northern Bank robbers forced someone else to do their dirty work. They terrified not only the bank's workers, but the workers' families as well. Their actions showed a brazen disregard for others. They come in at #3.
• What other security precautions do you think banks and the police need to take to prevent tiger kidnappings?

2 BOSTON ART

A real glimpse inside the Isabella Stewart Gardner Museum. The FBI has a $5 million reward for the return of all the stolen pieces of art.

THEFT

DATE: March 18, 1990

TARGET: Isabella Stewart Gardner Museum in Boston, Massachusetts

THE CRIME: Two bold thieves baffled police when they somehow scammed their way into a tightly guarded museum in the wee hours of the night.

THE LOOT: Rare pieces of art worth an estimated $300 million

One of the biggest art thefts in history took only two men and a little over an hour to pull off!

On March 18, 1990, two men somehow conned their way into the Isabella Stewart Gardner Museum in Boston. They showed up past midnight disguised as Boston police and actually managed to fool the museum's security guards into letting them in. These thieves didn't bother to cover their faces or bring any weapons along. They may have found out that there would only be two young and inexperienced security guards on duty the night of their planned crime. They walked right in and walked right back out with 13 pieces of art worth an estimated $300 million!

And the real Boston police? They had no clue the robbery was even taking place! Nobody found out about the heist until the next morning.

For getting away with such a daring heist, the Boston art thieves make it to #2 on our list.

BOSTON ART THEFT

CASING THE JOINT

The Gardner is a small museum. At night, the building is watched by two security guards. They take turns making rounds throughout the building and staffing the main security desk. At the desk, they watch the video monitors that feed images from the security cameras around the building. They also keep an eye on a computer that receives silent alerts from the motion detectors in the museum. Underneath the desk is the only alarm button in the museum that can alert the police of any emergencies.

 What was the main flaw in the museum's security system that allowed such a bold robbery?

THE PLAN

At 1:24 AM, one of the Gardner's security guards spotted two men on the museum's video monitor. It was the two thieves, wearing fake police jackets. They said they were answering a report of a "disturbance on the grounds" and needed to look inside the museum. The inexperienced security guards let them in. Within minutes, the thieves handcuffed and tied up the two guards with duct tape. After locking the guards in the museum's basement, they were now free to take whatever they wanted.

THE GETAWAY

At 2:28 AM, the thieves returned to the security office and put their last step of the plan in action. They removed the videotape from the recorder that had captured their images. They also stole the computer printout that showed what the motion detector had recorded. Thirteen minutes later, they walked out onto the empty street with their loot. It actually took them two trips to load all the stolen items into their getaway car. But they were lucky; there were no passersby to stop them.

Quick Fact

The museum's original owner, Mrs. Gardner, insisted in her will that nothing could ever be changed in the museum. So, after the robbery, museum staff kept the empty frames from the stolen art. In place of the paintings are tiny notes stating when the pieces were stolen.

What do you think the security guards could have done to protect themselves and the museum?

Vermeer's The Concert was stolen from the Gardner's Dutch Room.

The Expert Says...

" [Investigators] are baffled especially because the thieves, though bold and clever, were hardly meticulous professionals. They took no great pains to avoid being seen, nor were they careful to avoid damaging the masterpieces they were stealing. "

— Stephen Kurkjian, investigative reporter, *Boston Globe*

Anatomy OF an Art Heist

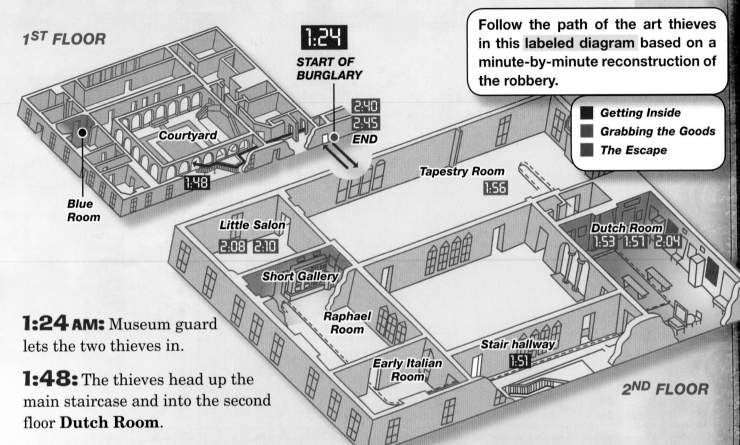

1ST FLOOR

1:24 START OF BURGLARY

2:40 2:45 END

Courtyard

1:48

Blue Room

Follow the path of the art thieves in this labeled diagram based on a minute-by-minute reconstruction of the robbery.

■ *Getting Inside*
■ *Grabbing the Goods*
■ *The Escape*

Tapestry Room **1:56**

Little Salon **2:08 2:10**

Short Gallery

Raphael Room

Early Italian Room

Stair hallway **1:51**

Dutch Room **1:53 1:51 2:04**

2ND FLOOR

1:24 AM: Museum guard lets the two thieves in.

1:48: The thieves head up the main staircase and into the second floor **Dutch Room**.

1:51: One thief leaves the room, tripping an alarm in the **stair hallway**. The thief goes through the **Early Italian Room** and into the **Little Salon**.

1:53: An alarm is tripped across the building in the **Dutch Room**, confirming that two thieves are at work in the museum.

1:56: An alarm sounds in the **Tapestry Room**, but nothing is later found missing.

1:57: At least one thief returns to the **Dutch Room**.

2:04: Both thieves now in the **Dutch Room**.

2:08: One thief goes to the **Early Italian Room** and then to the **Little Salon**.

2:10: Second thief heads to the **Little Salon**.

2:40: The inside and outside doors open and close within a minute of each other.

2:45: Inside door opens again, followed by the outside door. Investigators say this may indicate that the two thieves left separately within four minutes of one another.

Take Note

Like the Northern Bank robbery, a phony police disguise was the main element of the Boston art heist. But the art thieves take the #2 spot because they were shockingly bold — they didn't even try to avoid being seen. Even after they tripped the museum's internal alarms — allowing the security system to record their every move — they went ahead with their heist anyway.
• Many people later criticized the museum's security system. What would you change to better protect the museum?

5   4   3   2   1

Antwerp's diamond district is known for its state-of-the-art security systems.

IAMONDS

TARGET: Antwerp Diamond Center in Belgium, in Northwest Europe

THE CRIME: A crew of jewel thieves managed to learn how to perfectly overcome all of the various security systems designed to keep crooks out.

THE LOOT: More than $100 million worth of diamonds

On February 16, 2003, a crew of jewel thieves pulled one of the biggest heists of all time. For five hours, they went through the maximum security vault of Belgium's Antwerp Diamond Center. They were so loaded down with loot after breaking into 123 boxes that they left the last 37 untouched. The gems they managed to carry out of the building were worth more than $100 million.

The building and its vault were both supposedly protected by a series of state-of-the-art security features. But when police arrived on the scene, they found that all of these had been disabled.

Nobody knows how the thieves managed to get past and overcome such heavy and complicated security. It really should have been impossible! For that, this diamond heist takes the #1 spot on our list of most outrageous heists.

ANTWERP DIAMONDS

CASING THE JOINT

Antwerp, Belgium, is the diamond capital of the world! The city's "gem district" is protected by 24-hour police patrols and surveillance cameras. There are even metal barriers that prevent unauthorized vehicles from entering. Inside this heavily secured district is the large Antwerp Diamond Center. The Center itself requires special passes to enter and also has its own round-the-clock guards. The jewel of this building is its maximum-security underground vault. Here, 160 safe-deposit boxes hold all sorts of valuables — gold, cash, jewelry, and, of course, diamonds.

surveillance: *close observation*

Quick Fact

Around 80 percent of the world's diamonds pass through the Belgian city of Antwerp. Professional diamond buyers, diamond dealers, and jewelry manufacturers all come here to buy and sell their gems.

THE PLAN

Three years before the heist, the gang posed as a real business and rented an office in the Center. This was how they learned the ins and outs of the building's intricate security system. They even copied the master keys to the building! The night of the heist, they disabled the security system (including a motion detector and a light sensor) and simply let themselves in. Police aren't sure how they cracked the code to the vault, but they did. Once inside, the crew opened the safe-deposit boxes and went through the loot. They even stole records of authenticity that went along with the valuables they took, because this would make them easier to resell. Anything that could be easily traced they left behind.

THE GETAWAY

The gang made sure to cover all their bases upon their exit. They stole the videotape recordings from the security cameras and replaced them with copies of the previous night's footage. Then, they took the simplest and safest route out — via the building's underground garage, which had an exit that opened onto a street outside the diamond district. That brought them out onto the street one block away from the metal barriers, round-the-clock security guards, and the district's police station!

The Expert Says...

" [This was] a piece of genius in its simplicity, not in the least because the security system was so thoroughly analyzed. "

— Eric Sack, Antwerp's director of judicial services

? Take a look at how the criminals bypassed all of the different security devices in the Center. What changes do you think should be made to ensure that these devices won't be disabled so easily in the future?

ENTRANCE

ELEVATOR-4-1934

ELEVATOR-5-1935 15

16

10

8

7

6

ICE, ICE, Baby

The giant diamond seen here is the famous Lesotho Promise that was sold in Antwerp's diamond district.

8 Things You Didn't Know About Antwerp Diamonds

The jewel thieves who broke into the Antwerp Diamond Center chose their target for a reason. Check out this fact chart about Antwerp, the world's diamond trading capital!

1 Around 80% of the world's uncut diamonds are traded through Antwerp. That makes for 25 million carats of diamonds each year!

2 The Lesotho Promise, the 15th largest diamond ever discovered, was sold in October 2006 in Antwerp for $12.4 million. The 603-carat gem is the size of a golf ball — compare this to Victoria Beckham's engagement ring at three carats, or Catherine Zeta-Jones's whopper at 10 carats.

3 In the mid-1970s, Antwerp had 25,000 diamond cutters and polishers. Today, only 1,700 remain — and they cut only expensive stones.

4 Today, there are four diamond trading clubs in Antwerp. They employ around 30,000 people.

5 There's hardly any shade in Antwerp's diamond district! That's because the area's officials don't allow trees — trees would block the sight lines of the surveillance cameras everywhere.

6 In Antwerp, diamond dealers dash between their offices with their briefcases handcuffed to their hands.

7 Antwerp became the world's leader in the diamond industry because so much diamond trading and dealing occurred here. Fifty-five years ago, all of the world's diamond exchanges were located in Antwerp!

8 Antwerp's diamond days started back in 1447. This was where the world's earliest written record of diamond cutting took place.

Take Note

This heist didn't involve any force, violence, or drama. The gang simply walked into one of the most heavily guarded buildings in Antwerp's diamond district and walked out again — without any trouble or confrontation. We consider this inside job the most outrageous heist ever!

• Do you think this diamond heist deserves the #1 spot on our list of outrageous heists? If you don't, give your reasons and re-rank the list according to your own criteria!

5   4   3   2   1

We Thought …

Here are the criteria we used in ranking the 10 most outrageous heists.

The heist:
- Was a looting of a country's national treasures
- Involved lots of planning
- Threatened the lives of innocent people
- Featured a dangerous getaway
- Stumped police or security experts
- Was committed by robbers who were never caught
- Involved the use of sophisticated technology

Adolph Maffi

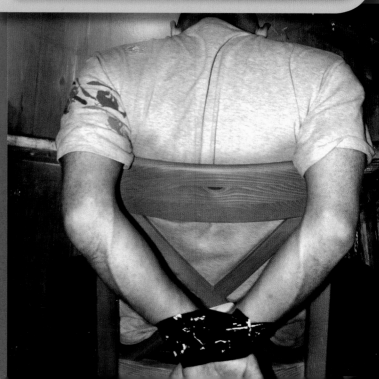